BASIC RU OF
GRAMMAr
ANSWER BOOK 4

Contents

Editor: Claire Ancell
Layout artist: Suzanne Ward

© 1996 Folens Limited, on behalf of the authors.
Every effort has been made to contact copyright holders of material used in this book. If any have been overlooked, we will be pleased to make any necessary arrangements.

British Library in Publication Data. A catalogue record for this book is available from the British Library.

First published 1996 by Folens Limited, Dunstable and Dublin.
Folens Limited, Albert House, Apex Business Centre, Boscombe Road, Dunstable, LU5 4RL, England.

ISBN 1 85276259-4

Printed in Great Britain by Colour Quest.

Nouns

A
1. joiner/carpenter
2. library
3. frog/toad
4. microscope
5. architect
6. cinema
7. unicorn
8. scissors

B
1. **Rover** the dog swam across the wide river.
2. **Fluffy** was playing happily with a ball of wool.
3. **Sam** enjoyed going to **Brighton**.
4. A truck towed the broken-down **Ford** car along the road.
5. **Sean Connery** appeared in many films as British spy **James Bond**.
6. We went to **York** to visit **Aunt Jane**.
7. **Jan** and **Mia** saw **Mr Singh** catch the thief.
8. The lion escaped from its cage in **Whipsnade Zoo**.
9. **Mrs Pierce** shouted loudly at the barking dog.
10. **Old Jock** walked slowly along **West Street**.

C Any suitable nouns for the groups shown.

Collective nouns

A
1. a flock of **sheep**
2. a pack of **cards**
3. a fleet of **ships**
4. a swarm of **bees**
5. a crowd of **people**
6. a squadron of **aeroplanes**
7. a herd of **cattle**
8. a library of **books**
9. a babble of **voices**
10. a wardrobe of **clothes**
11. a bunch of **flowers**
12. a clump of **grass**
13. a string of **beads**
14. a ream of **paper**
15. a team of **footballers**
16. a choir of **singers**
17. a school of **whales**
18. a crew of **sailors**
19. a pride of **lions**
20. a shoal of **fish**

B Any suitable collective nouns for the groups shown.

Basic Rules of Grammar: Answer Book 4

Groups and collective nouns

A
1. trees
2. fish
3. mountain ranges
4. oceans
5. countries/nations
6. cities
7. boats/sailing vessels
8. musical instruments
9. snakes
10. planets

B Any examples of interesting sentences using the phrases given.

C
1. bunch of **flowers/bananas/grapes**

2. parliament of **penguins**

3. hand of **bananas/cards**

4. nest of **vipers**

5. gaggle of **geese (on the ground)**

6. pod of **peas/whales**

7. swarm of **bees/insects**

8. rising of **larks**

9. litter of **piglets/cubs/pups**

10. congregation of **people/starlings**

11. skein of **wool/silk/geese (in flight)**

12. forest of **trees**

A

1. **A**t the end of every sentence there is a full stop.
2. **S**he is older than **I**.
3. **Y**esterday **S**hazia **S**ian was absent from school.
4. **I** have a baby brother named **A**lan.
5. **P**eaches and bananas are delicious fruits.
6. **S**aqib and **I** went to the cinema on **T**uesday.
7. **D**r **D**aly and **L**ord **C**arter live in **M**anchester.
8. **A**lankar and **R**aymond are in the library.
9. **W**e write in our diaries every day.
10. **I** hope you like our new office.
11. **I** have a friend called **M**anjinder.
12. **I** invited **A**nne to my party.
13. **L**ast **T**hursday the school team won the chess final.
14. **W**e do not go to school on **C**hristmas **D**ay.
15. **M**uslims all over the world celebrate **R**amadan.
16. **N**ovember comes between **O**ctober and **D**ecember.
17. **M**uriel's mother made pancakes on **S**hrove **T**uesday.
18. **M**y summer holidays lasted from **J**une to **S**eptember.
19. **W**e went to the seaside for the **E**aster **B**ank **H**oliday.
20. **I**n **A**merica the fourth of **J**uly is called **I**ndependence **D**ay.
21. **A**pril the first is called **A**pril **F**ools' **D**ay.
22. **P**eter's best friend was born on **N**ew **Y**ear's **D**ay.
23. **T**here are two songs that **I** like.
24. **I** wrote to **A**unt **J**eanette on **S**aturday.

Plurals

A
1. dog, **dogs**
2. eye, **eyes**
3. step, **steps**

B
1. circus, **circuses**
2. church, **churches**
3. bench, **benches**

C
1. lady, **ladies**
2. baby, **babies**
3. family, **families**

D
1. donkey, **donkeys**
2. valley, **valleys**
3. monkey, **monkeys**

E
1. half, **halves**
2. knife, **knives**
3. self, **selves**

F
1. foot, **feet**
2. mouse, **mice**
3. woman, **women**

G
1. radio, **radios**
2. patio, **patios**
3. cuckoo, **cuckoos**

H
1. potato, **potatoes**
2. volcano, **volcanoes**
3. hero, **heroes**

I
1. deer, **deer**
2. fish, **fish**
3. sheep, **sheep**

Pronouns

A Trevor received a new computer for Christmas. **He** had also got two games for **his** computer. Trevor couldn't wait to try **them**. First of all **he** put the 'Space Attack' disc in, but **it** would not load. **He** tried the other disc but **it** would not load either. **He** was furious. Just then, **his** father came into the room. Trevor told **him** that the games wouldn't load and **his** dad looked carefully at **them**. Suddenly **his** father laughed. "**They** are for a different make of computer. Never mind, I'll change **them** tomorrow!"

B When your child comes to St Thomas' School he **or she** will learn the basic skills of reading, writing and numeracy. He **or she** will need a pair of plimsolls for PE and a schoolbag for books and pencils. It will be helpful if all clothes have name labels. We hope your child will be happy at St Thomas' School.

Test 1

A
1. countries/nations
2. rivers
3. musical/stringed instruments
4. tools

B
1. a **pack** of wolves
2. a **school/pod** of whales
3. a **flock** of sheep
4. a **crowd** of people
5. a **bunch** of flowers
6. a **library** of books

C
1. hand, **hands**
2. pen, **pens**
3. elf, **elves**
4. brush, **brushes**
5. pear, **pears**
6. hoof, **hooves**
7. lorry, **lorries**
8. potato, **potatoes**
9. daisy, **daisies**
10. key, **keys**
11. cherry, **cherries**
12. child, **children**
13. shelf, **shelves**
14. leaf, **leaves**
15. adult, **adults**
16. mouse, **mice**
17. goose, **geese**
18. fungus, **fungi/funguses**
19. tomato, **tomatoes**
20. glass, **glasses**
21. cactus, **cacti/cactuses**
22. sheep, **sheep**
23. mummy, **mummies**
24. octopus, **octupi/octopuses**

D
Angelo ate an orange. **He** gave Peter an apple.

Then **they** saw Mr Harris in the garden.

He said, "Hello!" to **them**.

Basic Rules of Grammar: Answer Book 4

Comparative and superlative adjectives

A
1. old, **older**
2. warm, **warmer**
3. ancient, **more ancient**
4. fluffy, **fluffier**
5. delicious, **more delicious**
6. light, **lighter**
7. heavy, **heavier**
8. comfortable, **more comfortable**

B
1. revolting, **most revolting**
2. tuneful, **most tuneful**
3. easy, **easiest**
4. sad, **saddest**
5. early, **earliest**
6. stupid, **stupidest**
7. happy, **happiest**
8. straight, **straightest**
9. colourful, **most colourful**
10. speedy, **speediest**

Past tense

A 1. The bird **flitted** across the sky.

2. The woodlouse **crawled** under the stone.

3. The small butterfly **hovered** near the rose bushes.

4. The house spider **scurried** into its web.

5. The fat worm **wriggled** into its burrow.

6. The golden eagle **grabbed** the lamb in its talons.

B 1. She **wrote** a letter to her friend. She **has written** to her friend.
2. He **went** for a drive. He **has gone** to visit his aunt.
3. He **came** late last night. He **has come** at last.
4. He **gave** her a lovely present. He **has given** her a new car.
5. The hungry dog **ate** the meat. The dog **has eaten** its first meal in two days.
6. He **flew** to London. He **has flown** only once before.

C 1. Peter saw a colony of bats as he walked **past** the graveyard.
2. The crowd cheered as the queen drove **past**.
3. The proud eagle swooped **past** her nest.
4. Many days **passed** before my racing pigeon returned home.
5. They were bitten by mosquitos as they **passed** through the woods.
6. At half **past** eight the bus **passed** by my house.
7. The bird flew **past** in wide circles and **passed** over the marshy swamp.

A He ran **quickly** down the street. He looked **anxiously** left and right. **Fortunately** everything was quiet. He felt tired and rather unhappy to be running **away** so soon. He reached the crossroads and stopped. He started **again** and turned into the High Street. **Suddenly** he stopped. There was the sound of footsteps behind him. His heart beat **violently**. He was being followed!

B The gaps should be filled with suitable adverbs.

A
1. kind, **kindly**
2. suspicious, **suspiciously**
3. notable, **notably**
4. gentle, **gently**
5. quiet, **quietly**
6. mad, **madly**
7. light, **lightly**
8. last, **lastly**
9. silent, **silently**
10. bright, **brightly**

B
1. possible, **possibly**
2. manageable, **manageably**
3. valuable, **valuably**
4. suitable, **suitably**
5. reliable, **reliably**
6. noticeable, **noticeably**
7. terrible, **terribly**
8. miserable, **miserably**
9. horrible, **horribly**
10. legible, **legibly**
11. comfortable, **comfortably**
12. impossible, **impossibly**
13. reasonable, **reasonably**
14. visible, **visibly**
15. responsible, **responsibly**
16. incredible, **incredibly**

C Any sentences that include four of the adverbs from **B**.

Alphabetical order

A

1. To divide things up — **separate**
2. A soldier on guard — **sentry**
3. Someone who serves you — **servant**
4. Winter is one — **season**
5. More than two or three — **several**
6. After the first — **second**
7. You do this with a needle — **sewing**
8. To grab hold — **seize**
9. A seat — **settee**
10. Not thinking of others — **selfish**

B

season, second, seize, selfish, sentry, separate, servant, settee, several, sewing

C

Anderson, P
Anson, P
Brown, J
Burns, R
Burton, C
Butcher, B
Candy, B
Canova, J
Celini, R
Johnson, K

Jones, J
Paris, C
Parker, C
Pasternak, B
Patel, A
Summers, R
Sumner, B
Trimmer, R
Turner, S

Basic Rules of Grammar: Answer Book 4 © Folens

A Any suitable adjectives to make the sentences more interesting.

B

Adjective	Comparative	Superlative
big	bigger	**biggest**
happy	**happier**	happiest
sad	sadder	**saddest**
beautiful	**more beautiful**	**most beautiful**
revolting	more revolting	**most revolting**

C
1. I **gave** lots of presents.
2. The dog **ate** the food.
3. The thief **ran** away.
4. I **forgot** which way to go.
5. I **went** for a walk.

D
1. possible, **possibly**
2. comfortable, **comfortably**
3. tidy, **tidily**
4. happy, **happily**
5. terrible, **terribly**

E seat, seldom, send, service, settle, several

The full stop

A 1. The snow lay deep on the ground. It was very cold in the tents. Although the campers had sleeping bags they were not warm.

2. We agreed to meet at the shops. When I arrived Paul was not there. I waited for twenty minutes.

3. The robin gave the stick to the squirrel. He threw it to the frog. The frog took the stick in his mouth and dived into the pond.

4. A thick fog covered Dublin last night. Parts of the city were very badly affected. Motorists were advised to drive carefully.

5. A bad storm blew up at sea. All the fishing ships made for the harbour. The lighthouse-keeper was worried for their safety.

6. He caught the ball. He passed it to Jenny. She kicked it to Shane who slammed it into the back of the net.

7. She lived in a small cottage on the hillside. A small stream ran by the house. It would dry up in summertime.

8. Look for a safe place. Stop and wait. Look all around and listen before you cross the road.

B 1. One morning Peter and his hound went hunting red deer. They saw a beautiful lady. She wore a robe of silk. Her horse wore shoes of pure gold. He had never before seen such a beautiful lady.

2. William jumped on the white horse behind the princess. As the horse galloped away he waved goodbye to Peter and his hound. Soon they reached the edge of the sea. It opened before them and they passed through. He saw strange fish that no man had ever seen before.

Commas

A
1. On the table there is a telephone, a vase of flowers, a book and a key.
2. Through the window I can see a church, a car, a road, trees, clouds and a windmill.

B
1. On the table there is a knife, a plate, a cup of tea and a loaf of bread.
2. Through the window I can see clouds, a factory, a wall, a train and a railway bridge.

Commas

A 1. Rover, **the friendly old sheep dog**, barked at the strangers.

2. The Mississippi, **the longest river in America**, flows into the Gulf of Mexico.

3. We visited Norway, **a land of mountains and fjords**.

4. Susan, **my youngest sister**, is five today.

5. Mr Matthews, **the head teacher**, was not amused.

6. Liverpool, **a large city in England**, has two cathedrals.

B The sentences should each have a phrase added, giving extra information.

Apostrophes: possession

A Any two sentences about each of the pictures, using apostrophes to indicate possession.

B 1. The gobstopper stuck in the budgie's beak.

2. Brian's plan went wrong.

3. The tea spilled over Granny's pension book.

4. Dracula's teeth glinted in the moonlight.

5. Greta's breath came in short, nervous gasps.

A
1. Pig is to **piglet** as sheep is to lamb.
2. Dog is to **kennel** as hare is to form.
3. Caterpillar is to butterfly as **tadpole** is to frog.
4. Kitten is to cat as puppy is to **dog**.
5. Horse is to stable as cow is to **barn/byre**.
6. Paw is to dog as hoof is to **horse**.
7. Shoal is to herring as school is to **fish**.
8. Spider is to fly as cat is to **mouse**.

B
1. as blind as a **bat**
2. as graceful as a **swan**
3. as slow as a **snail**
4. as gentle as a **lamb**
5. as strong as a **horse**
6. as swift as a **hawk**
7. as hungry as a **wolf**
8. as brave as a **lion**
9. as wise as an **owl**

C
1. seal, sheep, skunk, **sparrow**, squirrel
   The only one that can fly.
2. pike, trout, **whale**, herring, cod
   The only mammal.
3. rabbit, badger, **otter**, fox, hare
   The only one that lives in water.
4. peach, pineapple, pear, **potato**, plum
   The only vegetable.
5. oyster, mussel, **octopus**, periwinkle, whelk
   The only one that is not a shellfish.
6. fir tree, yew tree, pine tree, **beech tree**
   The only one that is not an evergreen.
7. donkey, kangaroo, **mule**, ferret
   The only hybrid (animal bred from two different species).
8. magpie, **penguin**, cuckoo, robin, blackbird
   The only one that cannot fly.
9. stallion, filly, colt, **buffalo**, foal
   The only one that is not a horse.

Homophones

A
1. There is a hole in the **sole** of my shoe.
2. Have a **piece** of cake.
3. We had **cereal** for breakfast.
4. A basement can be called a **cellar**.
5. We use a **plumb** line to check that a line is vertical.
6. I live in a house with three **storeys**.
7. Electrical **currents** can be dangerous.
8. **Thyme** is a herb.
9. I will need some **coarse** sandpaper.

B
1. bored – fed up
   board – a plank of wood
2. scent – a pleasant smell
   sent – the past tense of send
3. steel – a metal
   steal – take something which belongs to someone else
4. stare – look hard at something or someone
   stair – steps
5. warn – tell about danger
   worn – well-used, past tense of wear
6. meddle – interfere
   medal – an award
7. write – make words or letters on paper
   right – correct, or opposite to left
8. whole – all
   hole – opening or hollow
9. allowed – permitted
   aloud – so that people can hear

10. waist – part of the body between the hips and ribs
    waste – no longer needed, or to throw away
11. mined – taken from under ground
    mind – brain
12. steak – meat
    stake – a sharp piece of wood driven into the ground
13. peace – calmness, or quiet
    piece – a part, or bit
14. source – where something starts
    sauce – a liquid to flavour food
15. sealing – closing
    ceiling – top part of a room
16. idol – something or someone that people worship
    idle – lazy

Basic Rules of Grammar: Answer Book 4   © Folens

Homophones

C Any sentences using the following homophones:

1. which
   witch

2. threw
   through

3. grown
   groan

4. air
   heir

5. pair
   pear

6. bare
   bear

Conjunctions

A **The Tunnel**

A new tunnel was planned **because** there was too much traffic for the only tunnel under the river. **Although** it would be useful, it would be expensive **because** a toll would have to be paid by drivers. **Therefore** local people protested about the toll **so** they were given special passes. Work was delayed for two months **because** there was a flood. **However** the flood went down **and** the workers soon made up for lost time.

B Any three sentences with the following conjunctions:

nevertheless   notwithstanding   despite

C although   because   however   so

Test 3

A
1. Fed up — **bored**
2. A metal — **steel**
3. The opposite of old — **new**
4. To speak out loud — **aloud**
5. A part of — **piece**

B
1. The book belonging to John.
   John's book
2. The books belonging to the children.
   the children's books
3. The biscuit belonging to the dog.
   the dog's biscuit
4. The biscuits belonging to the dogs.
   the dogs' biscuits

C
1. Mr Millar, **a rather old man**, walked slowly up the stairs.
2. Sarah, **a shy girl**, said nothing.
3. The building, **a big detached house**, was destroyed by fire.

D
1. The dog barked **so** the cat jumped over the fence.
2. The boy blushed **because** his trousers were badly torn.
3. It was raining **but** I still played football.

Synonyms

A

happy	sad
cackle	complain
cheer	grieve
chortle	grimace
chuckle	grizzle
giggle	groan
grin	grumble
laugh	moan
smile	scowl
smirk	sigh
snigger	whine
	whinge

B Any sentences using the following words:

cried   sobbed   cackled   laughed

C The words in red should be replaced with synonyms.

Example answers:

1.   I was **amused/surprised** to see no pictures in the gallery.

2.   Write in the **empty** space.

3.   The number is at the **bottom** of the page.

4.   He **looked** at the skateboard.

5.   The two countries were **joined** to make one.

6.   Swimming is **forbidden** in the lake.

D Any three sentences using verbs that can be used in different ways.

Similes

A
1. as clear as **crystal**
2. as heavy as **lead**
3. as steady as a **rock**
4. as light as a **feather**
5. as sharp as a **knife**
6. as good as **gold**
7. as quick as **lightning**
8. as flat as a **pancake**

B
1. The sweets were **as sweet as honey**.
2. The lime was **as sour as vinegar**.
3. He is **as round as a barrel**.
4. The leaves were **as green as grass**.
5. His face was **as white as snow**.
6. He was **as cool as a cucumber**.
7. She was **as hot as fire**.
8. She is **as thin as a rake**.

C Any suitable words to use as similes in the sentences shown.

Colloquialisms

A The sentences should be re-written showing the meanings of the colloquialisms. Example answers:

1. The audience **cheered loudly** at the end of the performance.
2. It was raining **heavily**.
3. Jane made a **quick run** to school.
4. James was **special to** his mother/his mother's **favourite**.
5. When the teacher talked about the visit the class **listened carefully**.
6. Mike and Sue were always **arguing**.
7. Carol's **heart beat quickly** when she heard the strange voice.
8. The detective **was suspicious** when the thief told him where he had got the silver cup from.
9. Mr Smith **did not tell his wife** about his plans.
10. After getting all his spellings wrong, Alan **had to be told his results**.

A

Patient:	Doctor, I've swallowed my pen.
Doctor:	That's OK. Use a pencil.

Patient:	Doctor, when I woke up this morning I swallowed my clock.
Doctor:	There's no need to be alarmed.

Patient:	Doctor, I'm nervous because this is my first operation.
Doctor:	I'm nervous too. It's the first operation I've done.

Doctor:	Have you had this before?
Patient:	Yes, doctor.
Doctor:	Well, you've got it again.

Patient:	Doctor, will I be able to play the guitar after my operation?
Doctor:	Of course.
Patient:	That's great! I've never been able to play it before!

Patient:	Doctor, no one listens to me.
Doctor:	Next please!

Patient:	Doctor, I've lost my memory.
Doctor:	When did that happen?
Patient:	When did what happen?

Patient:	Doctor, I think I've become invisible.
Doctor:	Who said that?

B   "Where have you been?" shouted my Dad. "What time of night do you call this?" I was very upset. When my Dad shouts at me I feel like crying. I feel such a baby. "I've been out with my friends," I said. I took care not to sound too cheeky because that makes Dad go mad. "And don't they have homes to go to," he asked, "or are you all out on the streets to see what trouble you can find?" "That's not fair," I cried. "We haven't done anything wrong. We only went to the youth club and played snooker." My Dad went red with anger.

"Look here young man, don't answer me back or I'll take that grin off your face. We have rules in this house," he went on, "and when I say you will be back here at ten that is what I mean."

A
1. "You look like a ghost," said Sarah.
2. The ghost replied, "That's because I am a ghost!"
3. Sarah screamed at the top of her voice, "A ghost!"
4. "You're deafening me!" exclaimed the ghost.
5. "Sorry," said Sarah.
6. "Are you really a ghost?" asked Sarah after a moment.
7. The ghost sighed, "What do you think?"
8. Sarah said, "I can see through you."
9. "What do you mean?" asked the ghost.
10. "I can see through the trick you're playing!" laughed Sarah.

B   A story made up using the above sentences and explaining how and why the trick was played on Sarah.

Dialogue

B Mr Jones looked at the car longingly. He liked its shape and its bright red paintwork, but he did not like the price tag on the windscreen. The salesman moved in for the kill.

"This is the car for you sir," said the salesman smoothly. "Only one owner, perfect condition and very easy on petrol."

"I don't know," said Mr Jones doubtfully. "It's not quite what I had in mind."

"I wouldn't touch this foreign rubbish if I were you sir," answered the salesman quickly. "They look good, but they're always letting you down, most unreliable."

"Still," muttered Mr Jones, "this is a bit expensive isn't it?"

"One year's guarantee, sir. Buy one of the others, you'll pay extra in repairs and service. This little beauty will run for years, no danger."

C A short dialogue making use of punctuation and paragraphs.

Test 4

A Ten different ways of saying **to speak**, for example:

mutter, shout, bellow, whisper, yell, stammer, mumble, grumble, whine, murmur.

B Completed similes. Example answers:

1. The snow was like **powder/a white blanket**.
2. The water was as cold as **ice**.
3. The fog was like **smoke/a grey blanket**.
4. The sun was as hot as **fire**.

C The colloquialisms should be replaced with words that have the same meaning.
Example answers:

1. We laughed **merrily/loudly**.
2. You need to **take great care** when climbing mountains.
3. **Look out** for wasps.
4. I won by **a tiny distance**.
5. He **only just** escaped.
6. He was going to dive from the top board but he **was too scared**.
7. Joe **was angry** when the children ruined his flower beds.
8. We tried to pursuade Mrs Jones to let us borrow her scissors, but she would not **change her mind**.

D Example answers to the questions:

1. "Nothing," answered the girl.
2. "I was helping my Mum," answered Sam.
3. "Yes please," answered the woman.
4. "It's a landscape," replied the artist.
5. "Over there please," replied the manager.

Basic Rules of Grammar: Answer Book 4

Put them in order

A 1. second, minute, hour, day, week
2. mouse, cat, sheep, cow, elephant
3. village, town, city, country, continent
4. spring, stream, river, sea, ocean
5. letter, word, sentence, page, chapter

B 1. strolled, walked, marched, jogged, ran
2. smiled, giggled, chuckled, laughed, guffawed
3. whispered, talked, shouted, shrieked, roared
4. draught, breeze, wind, gale, hurricane
5. molehill, mound, slope, hill, mountain
6. cold, cool, warm, hot, boiling
7. nervous, startled, alarmed, frightened, terrified
8. dinghy, boat, tug, ferry, liner

Ordering a story

A Ben was getting very excited as he looked out of the window.

They were approaching Manchester airport.

He could see houses and fields as the plane landed.

He was wondering if Aunt Mary would be there to meet him.

After he had collected his case Ben walked towards the exit.

Ben looked out at the sea of faces as he came out of the door.

Suddenly he saw the face he was searching for.

Aunt Mary was smiling and waving to him.

"Welcome to Manchester," she said.

Paragraphs

A   Paul is tall, dark and strong looking. He has dark hair, dark eyes and sun-tanned skin. He has a happy, friendly face and people like him.

Paul lives on a farm near a small town in Scotland. The farm is big and his father keeps sheep on the hillsides and cows for beef and grows crops. His home is near the mountains so he has a long way to go to meet his friends.

Paul loves the winter and likes to ski down the snowy, mountain slopes. When he cannot go to see his friends he spends his time making wooden models. Paul likes to listen to pop music and he has a lot of records.

B   Any three paragraphs about a famous person.

Test 5

A 1. March, May, August, October, December
     2. whisper, mutter, talk, shout, scream
     3. tiny, small, big, huge, colossal
     4. seed, seedling, sapling, tree

B 2. Sam woke early. It was still quite dark. He slipped quietly out of bed. Sam walked down the stairs, hoping they wouldn't creak. Then he opened the front door and made a dash for freedom.

C A description of Mrs Brown using the notes provided.

Homonyms

A   Example of suitable answers:

1. I cut my **hands** on a nail.

2. The clock has two **hands**.

3. Here is a **set** of golf clubs.

4. The sun will **set** at seven o'clock.

5. Two prize fighters will **box** tonight.

6. Here is a **box** of chocolates.

7. Please **ring** the bell.

8. She has a **ring** on each finger.

9. We will **skip** this page and go on to the next one.

10. I can **skip** with a rope.

B
1. not heavy and pale   **light**
2. to leave a stationary car and a place to play   **park**
3. a small animal and part of a computer   **mouse**
4. a plant and to skip on one foot   **hop**

C   Any sentences that show two meanings for each word:

1. grave   2. spring   3. rest   4. post

Verbs made from nouns

A televise, **television**
assassinate, **assassin**

liquify, **liquid**
victimise, **victim**

B 1. peace, **pacify**
2. radius, **radiate**
3. pursuit, **pursue**

4. saliva, **salivate**
5. package, **pack**

C 1. liking, **like**
carriage, **carry**

marriage, **marry**
carvery, **carve**

2. repetition, **repeat**
education, **educate**

alliance, **ally**
instruction, **instruct**

3. attraction, **attract**
cleaner, **clean**

radiation, **radiate**
teacher, **teach**

4. selection, **select**
eraser, **erase**

choice, **choose**
election, **elect**

Prefixes

Page 44

A 1. supernatural
2. supermarket
3. superhuman
4. supercilious
5. superfluous

6. superficial
7. superior
8. superabundant
9. superimpose
10. superpower

B superb

C supervisor

D superintendant

28   *Basic Rules of Grammar: Answer Book 4*   © Folens

Suffixes

A Once there was a **selfish** giant. He lived in a big castle. He did not like children playing in his garden. He hated their **childish** laughter. He was a very **foolish** giant because he became very sad and lonely in his freezing castle without any friends. Then one day he saw a small child sitting in the branches of a tree. The garden brightened up and flowers began to grow. The children began to creep back in a **sheepish** way into the garden. The giant realised how **foolish** he had been and was delighted to hear the **childish** voices around him. With a **tigerish** roar of laughter, he beckoned to them all to come in and play.

B Examples of dictionary definitions for the words listed:

1. **selfish** – caring only about yourself
2. **feverish** – suffering from a high temperature, or very excited
3. **sheepish** – embarrassed
4. **fiendish** – cruel or evil
5. **childish** – immature, or like a child
6. **tigerish** – fierce
7. **elfish** – small, light and graceful
8. **churlish** – surly
9. **Finnish** – from Finland
10. **babyish** – immature, or like a baby
11. **waspish** – sharp-tempered
12. **girlish** – like a girl
13. **foolish** – silly
14. **boyish** – like a boy
15. **Turkish** – from Turkey
16. **impish** – mischievous

Suffixes

A
1. teacher
2. sculptor
3. pianist
4. sailor
5. typist
6. driver
7. politician
8. cellist
9. conductor

B
1. A person from London. **Londoner**
2. A person from Venice. **Venetian**
3. A person from Darwin. **Darwinian**
4. A person from Boston. **Bostonian**

C
1. A flautist plays the flute.
2. An escapologist escapes from things.
3. A humanist is interested in humans, and not in a god.
4. A Buddhist worships Buddha.
5. An archaeologist looks for ancient remains.
6. A philatelist collects stamps.
7. A Mancunian comes from Manchester.
8. An Evertonian supports Everton Football Club.
9. An Austrian comes from Austria.
10. An Italian comes from Italy.
11. A Liverpudlian comes from Liverpool.
12. A physician is a doctor.
13. An undertaker organises funerals.
14. An adviser gives advice.
15. A producer produces things like television programmes, food and factory goods.
16. A publisher produces books.
17. A lecturer gives talks.
18. An editor gets books ready for publication.

Syllabication

A rattle, unicorn, unhappy, somebody, happy, nevertheless, invisible, personality, hover, position, responsibility, general, unbelievable, publishing, exercise, illustration, computer

B

One syllable	Two syllables	Three syllables
bank dream please square band	flower dozen extra bonus peaceful oblong blameless	pastrami hexagon petrify plantation construction adjacent radius overjoyed triangle potato

Four syllables	Five syllables	
triangular politician hexagonal eliminate elevation diagonally horizontal vertically	underestimate quadrilateral	

Test 6

A
1. Matched and healthy.   **fit**

2. Pull and use a pencil to make a picture.   **draw**

3. A hill and a direction for descending.   **down**

4. An animal and to follow.   **dog**

5. A curved shape and a weapon with arrows.   **bow**

B
1. case, **encase**
2. compass, **encompass**
3. liquid, **liquify/liquefy**
4. beauty, **beautify**

C
1. realisation, **realise**
2. mower, **mow**
3. cultivation, **cultivate**
4. entry, **enter**

D Any five words that begin with the prefixes **in**, **ex** and **un**.

E Any five words that end with the suffixes **ish**, **ful**, and **or**.

F The chart should be completed with words of the given numbers of syllables.